THE
DAD'S
BBQ
COOKBOOK

THE DAD'S BBQ COOKBOOK

An Hachette UK Company
www.hachette.co.uk

Summersdale Publishers
Part of Octopus Publishing Group Limited
Carmelite House
50 Victoria Embankment
LONDON
EC4Y 0DZ
UK

www.summersdale.com

This FSC® label means that materials used for the product have been responsibly sourced

MIX
Paper | Supporting responsible forestry
FSC® C016973
www.fsc.org

The authorized representative in the EEA is Hachette Ireland, 8 Castlecourt Centre, Dublin 15, D15 XTP3, Ireland (email: info@hbgi.ie)

Printed and bound in China

ISBN: 978-1-83799-499-1

Substantial discounts on bulk quantities of Summersdale books are available to corporations, professional associations and other organizations. For details contact general enquiries: telephone: +44 (0) 1243 771107 or email: enquiries@summersdale.com.

THE
DAD'S
BBQ
COOKBOOK

SWEET AND SAVOURY RECIPES
FOR THE ULTIMATE
BBQ SPREAD

SAM
BROOKS

summersdale

CONTENTS

INTRODUCTION
7

BBQ 101
8

BBQ TIPS AND TRICKS
11

CONVERSIONS AND MEASUREMENTS
15

RECIPE SYMBOLS
17

MEAT, FISH AND VEGGIE GRILLS
19

SAUCES, MARINADES AND RUBS
73

SIDE DISHES
93

SWEET TREATS
117

INTRODUCTION

Welcome to *The Dad's BBQ Cookbook*, the book that demystifies the smoky and delicious world of chargrilled food. Whether you're a seasoned pro or a first-time flipper, this book has all the tips and tricks any BBQ aficionado worth their salt and pepper needs to know.

Shake up your menu with over 50 mouth-watering recipes, from BBQ staples like kebabs, wings and burgers, to sides, sauces and desserts that will make your gathering one to remember.

So, get ready to flip those burgers, sizzle those steaks and expertly char those veggies – in no time you'll be the envy of all your friends as you handle the heat and do it with style.

On your marks, get set, GRILL!

BBQ 101
CHARCOAL vs GAS BBQ

A **charcoal grill** is one of the most popular kinds of BBQ. It is generally cheaper than a gas grill, and cooking over coals allows you to get that classic smoky BBQ flavour. However, it can be trickier to cook on, as you can't control the heat as easily. A **gas grill** is the no-fuss option. It's quick to heat up and easier than a charcoal grill to cook food with precision, but they tend to be more expensive.

CHOOSING YOUR CHARCOAL

The main choice is between **lump charcoal** and **briquettes**. **Lump charcoal** is one of the most natural forms of charcoal you can buy, and is preferred among BBQ connoisseursv as it heats quickly, burns hot and has that coveted smoky wood flavour. However, it can be expensive, and it also burns quickly, so if you are cooking for more than 45 minutes, you may need to add more charcoal to the grill to keep the heat up. **Briquettes** are charcoal plus other ingredients, such as sodium nitrate, which help the charcoal to burn more steadily. They are cheaper than lumps, and they maintain a high, even temperature for a longer time, so they're slightly easier to use. In a nutshell, lumps are the "organic" version of charcoal, and briquettes are more cost-effective – but both will give you an excellent, smoky BBQ to be proud of.

LIGHTING THE GRILL

If lighting a gas BBQ, follow the instructions in the user manual.

If lighting with charcoal, first remove the cooking grill. Place some charcoal at the bottom of the BBQ, along with two or three natural firelighters (use more or less depending on how much charcoal you're using). Then build a rough pyramid shape on top of this bottom layer with more charcoal. Use long matches to light the firelighters, and leave to burn for 20–30 minutes. When the coals are covered in white ash and glowing red, they are ready. Use a long-handled, heatproof implement, such as a charcoal rake, to arrange the coals into position for cooking (see the BBQ set-up on the next page).

BBQ SET-UP

There are lots of ways to set up your grill, but the most versatile is the two-zone fire. This means making a sloping pile of charcoal on one side of the grill, creating a high heat at one end, a medium heat in the middle and a low heat on the opposite end of the grill. This gives you a range of temperatures on your grill, which gives you more control over your cooking and also allows you to cook different kinds of food at the same time.

You can create this effect on a gas BBQ with three or more burners by turning on all but one of the burners. The burners that are switched on should range from high to medium heats (high at one end, medium in the middle), and the end where the burner is off will be the area of low heat.

The recipes in this book refer to high, medium and low heats, which refer to the high, medium and low heat areas on a two-zone fire.

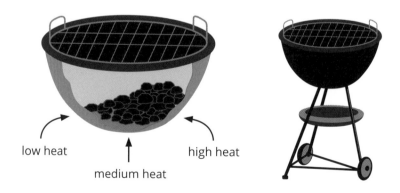

low heat

medium heat

high heat

BBQ TIPS AND TRICKS

ESSENTIAL BBQ TOOLS

- **Long-handled tongs x 2** – one set is for handling raw meat; the other is for handling cooked meat.

- **Spatulas or fish slices x 2** – these are useful if you are cooking a lot of burgers. You will need one for the raw meat and one for the cooked meat.

- **Metal or bamboo skewers** – your key piece of kit for kebabs.

- **Trays or plates** – make sure you have plenty of clean plates or trays on hand ready for your cooked meat.

- **Long matches** – for lighting the fire starters without risk of burning your fingers.

- **Oven or BBQ gloves** – to protect you from the heat.

- **Apron** – to protect your clothes from spitting, hot fat.

- **Basting brush** – useful for applying marinade or sauce to food as it cooks.

- **Meat thermometer** – helps to ensure that meat is cooked all the way through.

BBQ TEMPERATURE HACK

Here's a quick way to tell if your BBQ is up to temperature, and how hot each area of your grill is. Hold your palm 12 cm (5 in.) away from the grill and time how long you can hold it there before it becomes too hot:

- **Low heat** – 8–10 seconds

- **Medium heat** – 5–7 seconds

- **High heat** – 2–4 seconds

COOKING IMITATION MEAT

- As long as there are no elements of the food that can slip through the grill (such as beans in bean burgers) and there aren't instructions for the food not to be grilled, imitation meat can usually be cooked on the BBQ without trouble.

- Lightly oil or grease imitation meat products to prevent them sticking to the grill.

- As imitation meat is plant-based, it only needs to be grilled to the point where it is well heated throughout (unlike real meat, which needs to be heated for a longer time to cook it properly) – usually over a medium heat.

- If you're cooking for both meat eaters and non-meat eaters on the same grill, cook the non-meat items on a layer of tinfoil to avoid cross-contamination, and make sure you use different utensils, trays and plates to handle the food.

AVOIDING FLARE-UPS

A flare-up is a sudden burst of flame on the grill. Usually a flare-up is caused by fat dripping on to the coals, so they are an inevitable part of grilling and not necessarily bad. However, if the flames last for more than a couple of seconds, if they spread across the grill or if they start to produce black smoke and soot, not only can this ruin your cooking, but it also becomes dangerous.

To lower the risk of flare-ups:

- Keep your BBQ out of the wind.

- Remove excess fat from your meat.

- If you're applying an oily marinade, add it slowly and sparingly.

- Keep your grill clean.

SOME NOTES ON SAFETY

- Always read the instructions for the kind of BBQ that you are using to ensure that you're using it safely.

- Ensure that you position your BBQ in an open space away from overhanging trees and objects.

- Make sure nothing flammable dangles over the grill (e.g. sleeves, apron strings, hair, etc.).

- Have a bucket of sand or a grease-fire extinguisher on hand for emergencies.

- When cooking meat, always ensure that it is steaming hot throughout, that there is no pink meat visible in the thickest part, and that the juices run clear.

- If you do experience an extended flare-up, turn off the burners and gas cylinder of a gas grill, or pour a bucket of sand over a charcoal grill.

CONVERSIONS AND MEASUREMENTS

If you don't want to use metric measurements and need some basic conversions handy, refer back to the below:

Metric	Imperial
25 g	1 oz
60 g	2 oz
85 g	3 oz
115 g	4 oz
255 g	9 oz

Metric	Imperial
15 ml	0.5 fl oz
30 ml	1 fl oz
75 ml	2.5 fl oz
120 ml	4 fl oz
270 ml	9 fl oz

MEAT TEMPERATURES

We recommend using a meat thermometer to be extra certain that your meat is cooked before serving. Make sure you insert the thermometer into the middle of the thickest part of the meat and that you're not touching any bone or gristle. Then check that your meat has reached the following temperatures:

Meat:
Chicken: 75°C (167°F)
Lamb: 71°C (160°F)
Pork: 75°C (167°F)
Beef:
  Rare: 50°C (122°F)
  Medium: 63°C (145°F)
  Well done: 71°C (160°F)

Seafood:
White fish and salmon:
63°C (145°F)
Tuna: 52°C (126°F)
Scallops: 50°C (122°F)
Squid: 71°C (160°F)

RECIPE SYMBOLS

Look for the following symbols to find out whether a recipe is suitable for vegetarians or vegans*:

 Vegan

 Vegetarian

*Where processed products (e.g. ketchup) are used in the ingredients, always check specific brand details to ensure compatibility with a vegan diet.

MEAT, FISH AND VEGGIE GRILLS

Ribs with whisky glaze • Steak with peppercorn sauce • Jerk pork belly with mango salsa • Grilled pork and pineapple in a honey glaze • Marinated lamb skewers • Chicken and Mediterranean vegetable kebabs • Tandoori chicken skewers • BBQ honey chicken wings • Grilled Cajun chicken • Classic cheeseburger • Chicken and bacon burger • Classic BBQ sausage in a wholemeal bun • Hot dogs loaded with bacon, onions and peppers • Bacon and mozzarella sandwiches • Grilled squid with Thai dipping sauce • Seared tuna steak with soy sauce • Sweet chilli prawns • Grilled trout with new potatoes and cherry tomatoes • BBQ scallops • Cedar-smoked salmon • Grilled halloumi burger with yogurt mint sauce • Asian tofu burger • Cheesy portobello mushrooms • Grilled avocado stuffed with tomatoes and ricotta cheese • Mixed vegetable and BBQ seitan skewers • Grilled cauliflower steak

19

RIBS WITH WHISKY GLAZE

Bring the taste of the Deep South to your very own backyard with this easy recipe.

METHOD

Preheat oven to 160°C/320°F/gas mark 3.

Carefully remove membrane and excess fat from the ribs.

Mix the rub ingredients, then apply to the ribs with clean hands. Add as much as will stick, then discard the excess.

Transfer ribs to a roasting tin (approx. 30 cm (12 in.) long), then pour over 500 ml water, or enough to fill a quarter of the pan. Cover with foil and roast for 1–1.5 hours, until the meat is tender. Remove from oven.

Meanwhile, prepare the BBQ.

When the ribs are done, remove from the tin, pat dry and place on the grill on a low to medium heat, bone-side down. Cook for 15 minutes, turning every few minutes.

After this, baste both sides with the BBQ whisky glaze and continue to turn every couple of minutes. Keep basting and turning until the sauce has adhered to the ribs, and the meat is tender.

Serve immediately.

INGREDIENTS

12 spare ribs
 (approx. 1 kg)
Whisky glaze
 (see page 75)

For the rub:

1 heaped tbsp
 brown sugar
2 tsp salt
2 tsp ground
 black pepper
2 tsp paprika
2 tsp garlic granules
½ tsp chilli
 (or more to taste)

STEAK WITH PEPPERCORN SAUCE

With these bad boys, it's "fine dining meets epic BBQ food".

METHOD

Remove the steaks from the fridge, cover and allow them to come to room temperature (at least 30 minutes).

Prepare the BBQ.

Lightly brush the steaks with oil and season with salt and pepper to taste. Then place the steaks on the grill over a medium–high heat.

Cook for 3–4 minutes on each side (slightly less for a rare steak, slightly longer for a well-done steak).

You can test when the steak is done by touch. A rare steak will be soft to the touch. Medium rare is slightly firmer, but still with red juices. A medium steak is fairly firm to the touch with brown juices. Well-done steak will be completely firm and with brown juices.

When the steaks are done, remove from the grill, place them on a warm plate, cover with foil and leave for 5–10 minutes to rest.

Serve with a side of peppercorn sauce.

INGREDIENTS
2 thick sirloin steaks
2-3 tbsp olive oil
Salt and pepper,
 to taste
Shop-bought
 peppercorn
 sauce, to serve

JERK PORK BELLY WITH MANGO SALSA

For this recipe, you will need a BBQ with a lid in order to cook that pork belly low 'n' slow.

METHOD

Place all the marinade ingredients in a saucepan over a low heat. Stir until the sauce has thickened slightly. Leave it to cool.

Put the pork joint in a roasting tin or shallow dish. Pour half of the marinade over the pork and work it in with clean hands. Cover and leave to marinate in the fridge for 2 hours or overnight.

Prepare the BBQ. Meanwhile, take the pork out of the fridge to bring it to room temperature.

Place the pork skin-side down over the lowest heat on the grill. Put the lid down and leave it for 15 minutes, checking at intervals to make sure it isn't burning. Turn the pork over, close the lid and cook for another 15 minutes. Repeat twice more, so the pork has cooked for an hour.

When the meat is done, remove from the grill, cover and allow it to rest for 15–20 minutes.

Serve with some of the reserved marinade and a side of mango salsa.

SERVES: 4

INGREDIENTS
500 g pork belly joint
Mango salsa
  (see page 97)

For the jerk marinade:
1 tbsp jerk seasoning
2 cloves garlic, minced
3 tbsp soy sauce
2 tbsp vegetable oil
2 tbsp vinegar
3 tbsp orange juice

GRILLED PORK AND PINEAPPLE IN A HONEY GLAZE

A little bit sweet, a little bit salty, but a whole lot of delicious.

METHOD

Combine the glaze ingredients in a saucepan. Bring to the boil, then simmer for 5 minutes, stirring constantly. Adjust flavours to taste.

Prepare the BBQ. Meanwhile, drain the pineapple rings.

Place the pork chops over a medium–high heat. Cook until the underside is no longer pink (about a minute), then turn and cook the other side.

Gently brush a layer of glaze on both sides of each chop and cook for approx. 7 minutes on each side. In the last few minutes of cooking, brush on more of the glaze if desired.

Remove from the grill, cover and allow to rest for 5–10 minutes. Meanwhile, put the pineapple rings on a medium heat until char marks appear. Turn and repeat.

Serve immediately.

INGREDIENTS
4 pork chops
220-g tin pineapple
  rings

For the honey glaze:
2 tbsp ketchup
1 tbsp Worcestershire
  sauce
5 tbsp runny honey
1 tsp balsamic vinegar
4 cloves garlic, minced
2 tsp soy sauce
½ tsp chilli powder

MARINATED LAMB SKEWERS

Get a taste of the Mediterranean with these herby lamb kebabs.

METHOD

Trim the fat off the lamb and chop into chunks.

Mix the remaining ingredients in a large bowl. Add the lamb and mix well so each piece is well coated. Cover the bowl, refrigerate and allow to marinate for at least 4 hours, or overnight.

Prepare the BBQ.

If using bamboo skewers, soak them in water for at least 10 minutes, until saturated, to avoid them burning on the heat.

Thread the lamb on to the skewers and cook for 10–12 minutes on a medium heat, turning occasionally.

Serve immediately.

SERVES: 4-5

INGREDIENTS

750 g lamb leg
  or shoulder
80 ml olive oil
2 tsp oregano
1 tsp rosemary
½ tsp thyme
Juice of 2 lemons
3 cloves garlic, minced
½ tsp salt

CHICKEN AND MEDITERRANEAN VEGETABLE KEBABS

Chicken and veggies are a winning combo every time – especially when perfectly charred and served with a drizzle of lemon or lime.

METHOD

Chop the mushrooms into thick slices. Deseed and chop the pepper, and chop the red onion into large chunks.

If using bamboo skewers, soak them in water for at least 10 minutes, until saturated, to avoid them burning on the heat. Thread the chicken, mushroom, pepper and onion on to the skewers. Brush lightly with olive oil and sprinkle with salt. Cover and put to one side at room temperature.

Prepare the BBQ.

Place the skewers over a medium heat for 10–15 minutes, turning occasionally. When cooked, the juices of the chicken should run clear.

Serve immediately with lemon or lime wedges, ketchup and fresh rosemary if desired.

SERVES: 4-5

INGREDIENTS

400 g chicken, diced
5 small mushrooms
1 red pepper
1 red onion
Olive oil
Pinch salt
Lemon or lime
  wedges (optional)
Ketchup (optional)
Fresh rosemary
  (optional)

TANDOORI CHICKEN SKEWERS

Spice up your kebabs with this easy recipe.

METHOD

In a large bowl, add the tandoori rub, lemon juice and yogurt and mix well. Add the chicken and stir until each piece is well coated. Cover, refrigerate and leave to marinate for 4 hours or overnight.

Prepare the BBQ. If using bamboo skewers, soak them in water for at least 10 minutes, until saturated, to avoid them burning on the heat.

Thread the chicken on to the skewers. Place each skewer on the grill over a medium heat and cook for 10–15 minutes, turning occasionally. When cooked, the juices of the chicken should run clear.

Serve immediately.

MAKES:
2–3 skewers

INGREDIENTS
200 g chicken, diced
6 tsp tandoori rub
 (see page 90)
Juice of 1 lemon
60 g plain yogurt

BBQ HONEY CHICKEN WINGS

This is sticky-sweet, finger-licking comfort food at its very finest – and a real BBQ treat.

METHOD

Mix the brown sugar, garlic granules and salt in a small bowl and rub this over the chicken wings with clean hands. Cover and leave in the fridge for at least 30 minutes for the flavours to develop.

Combine the remaining ingredients in a saucepan to make the glaze. Bring to the boil, then simmer for 5 minutes, stirring constantly. Adjust flavours to taste.

Prepare the BBQ.

Place the wings over a medium–high heat on the BBQ and grill until the skins are brown and beginning to crisp, turning occasionally – about 5 minutes. Then move the wings to a medium heat for another 8–10 minutes, turning frequently. In the last few minutes, brush on the BBQ honey glaze and keep turning, adding more sauce if desired.

Serve immediately.

INGREDIENTS

8 large chicken wings
  (or 10 smaller wings)
1 tsp brown sugar
1 tsp garlic granules
1 tsp salt
2 tbsp ketchup
1 tbsp Worcestershire
  sauce
5 tbsp runny honey
1 tsp balsamic vinegar
4 cloves garlic, minced
2 tsp soy sauce
½ tsp chilli powder

GRILLED CAJUN CHICKEN

This is an easy way to add a bit of a kick to your chicken.

METHOD

Brush the chicken drumsticks lightly with oil. Then, with clean hands, rub them all over with the Cajun rub.

Prepare the BBQ.

Place the drumsticks over a medium heat and cook for 15–20 minutes, turning occasionally. When cooked, the juices of the chicken should run clear.

Serve immediately.

INGREDIENTS
8 chicken drumsticks
2 tbsp olive oil
4 tsp Cajun rub
 (see page 89)

CLASSIC CHEESEBURGER

You can't go wrong with this true BBQ classic.

METHOD

Add all the burger ingredients to a bowl and mix thoroughly. With clean hands, divide the mixture into four and shape each portion into a burger patty shape. Cover and set to one side (refrigerate if not using straight away).

Prepare the BBQ.

Place the burger patties over a high heat and cook for 3–4 minutes. Flip each burger and cook for another 3–4 minutes. Remove from the grill, cover and allow to rest for 5 minutes.

Meanwhile, slice the burger buns in half and place them flat-side down on the grill over a medium heat. Cook until the bottom of the buns are lightly toasted.

Assemble the burgers: for each one, layer the burger, cheese, onion, tomato and lettuce inside the bun, adding ketchup if desired, and serve immediately.

MAKES:
4 burgers

INGREDIENTS

For the burger patties:
500 g lean minced beef
1 red onion, grated finely
1 tsp garlic granules
1 tsp mixed herbs
1 egg, whisked
½ tsp salt
½ tsp ground black pepper

For the buns:
4 burger buns
4 slices American cheese
½ red onion, sliced
1 large tomato, sliced
4 large lettuce leaves, or
  other salad leaves of choice
Ketchup (optional)

CHICKEN AND BACON BURGER

Juicy chicken, salty bacon and sharp pickles make these burgers a meal to remember.

METHOD

Wrap the chicken breasts loosely in baking paper and place them on a stable work surface. Tenderize the meat by hitting it with a meat tenderizer or a rolling pin a few times, until the meat is an even thickness.

Whisk the oil, vinegar and lemon juice in a shallow dish, then add the chicken. Stir to coat, then cover and allow to marinate in the fridge for 30 minutes.

Prepare the BBQ.

Place the chicken on a medium heat and cook for 6–7 minutes. Then flip and cook for another 6–7 minutes.

Once the chicken has been flipped, add your bacon to the grill over the lowest heat possible, turning occasionally, and cook for 7 minutes, or until it is crisp at the edges.

In the last few minutes of cooking, slice the buns in half and place them flat-side down on a low heat to gently toast them, if desired.

Assemble the burgers: layer the lettuce, chicken, bacon and gherkins, if desired, inside the buns and serve.

MAKES:
2 burgers

INGREDIENTS
2 large chicken breasts
3 tbsp olive oil
1 tsp balsamic vinegar
1 tsp lemon juice
4 rashers bacon
2 brioche buns
2 large lettuce leaves,
    or other salad
    leaves of choice
Pickled gherkins,
    sliced (optional)

CLASSIC BBQ SAUSAGE IN A WHOLEMEAL BUN

A simple recipe for the all-American classic.

METHOD

Prepare the BBQ.

Brown the sausages over a high heat for 1–2 minutes, turning continuously. Then move the sausages to a low heat. Cook for a further 10–15 minutes, turning occasionally, until there is no pink on the insides and juices run clear.

Serve immediately in a wholemeal bun with mustard drizzled on top.

MAKES:
4 bunned sausages

INGREDIENTS

4 large sausages
4 wholemeal
  hot dog buns
Mustard, to serve

HOT DOGS LOADED WITH BACON, ONIONS AND PEPPERS

Upgrade your hot dogs to smokin'-hot hot dogs with these tasty toppings.

METHOD

Chop the onion into large chunks. Take a large piece of kitchen foil (20–30 cm (8–12 in.)) and brush one side lightly with olive oil. Put the chopped onion inside and loosely wrap the foil around it, so you have a small pouch.

Prepare the BBQ.

Put the foil pouch of onions over a medium heat and cook for 15 minutes, or until caramelized. When they are done, put them on the lowest heat on the grill to keep warm. Meanwhile, place the frankfurters over a medium heat and cook for 8–9 minutes, turning them every 1–2 minutes, until they have char marks on all sides.

After you turn the frankfurters the first time, put the bacon on the grill over the lowest heat, turning occasionally, and cook for 7 minutes, or until crisp at the edges.

Assemble the hot dogs: cut the buns down the middle and add one frankfurter, one rasher of bacon and a serving of onions to each bun. Top with green pepper and serve.

MAKES:
4 hot dogs

INGREDIENTS
1 onion
1 tbsp olive oil
4 frankfurters
4 rashers bacon
4 hot dog buns
1 green pepper,
 deseeded and diced

BACON AND MOZZARELLA SANDWICHES

There's nothing better than a grilled sandwich – unless it's a grilled sandwich done on the barbie.

METHOD

Tear the mozzarella ball into pieces and set to one side.

Prepare the BBQ.

Put the bacon on the grill over the lowest heat, turning occasionally, and cook for 7 minutes, or until it is crisp at the edges. Remove from the grill.

Lay out the slices of bread (buttered on the outside). Put two rashers of bacon on the base of each sandwich and top with pieces of mozzarella. Then close the sandwiches with the remaining slices of bread.

Place them on the grill over a medium heat. Cook for 2–3 minutes on each side, or until char marks form and the bread is toasted.

Serve immediately, with a simple side salad if desired.

MAKES:
3 sandwiches

INGREDIENTS
1 large mozzarella ball
6 rashers bacon
6 slices crusty bread
1 tbsp butter
Side salad, to serve
  (optional)

GRILLED SQUID WITH THAI DIPPING SAUCE

Fragrant, light, sharp-and-salty deliciousness!

METHOD
Whisk the sauce ingredients together until the sugar has dissolved. Set to one side.

Prepare the BBQ.

Pat the squid dry and remove as much of the moisture as possible from the surface. Then lightly oil the squid and place it on the grill over the highest heat possible. Cook for 2 minutes on each side, until char marks begin to appear.

Remove from the grill, slice into pieces and serve immediately with the dipping sauce.

SERVES: 2-3

INGREDIENTS
200 g squid tubes
1 tbsp olive oil

For the dipping sauce:
2 tbsp soy sauce
1 tbsp fish sauce
1 tsp lime
½ tsp rice vinegar
½ tsp brown sugar
Pinch chilli flakes
1 red chilli, deseeded and chopped

SEARED TUNA STEAK WITH SOY SAUCE

Try serving these steaks with a side of grilled green vegetables for an extra-special touch.

METHOD

Mix the oil and lemon juice in a shallow container and add the tuna steaks. Stir to coat, then cover, refrigerate and leave to marinate for 30 minutes.

Prepare the BBQ.

Sprinkle each tuna steak with salt and pepper to taste, then place on the grill over a medium heat for 4 minutes, or until char marks appear. Turn each steak over and cook for another 4 minutes.

Transfer to a plate and sprinkle the steaks with sesame seeds. Serve with a side of soy sauce.

INGREDIENTS
2 tbsp olive oil
2 tsp lemon juice
2 x 100-g tuna steaks
Pinch salt
Pinch pepper
1 tbsp black
   sesame seeds
Soy sauce, to serve

SWEET CHILLI PRAWNS

Bring some zing to your grill with these bright, spicy prawn skewers.

METHOD

Put the sweet chilli marinade in a large bowl, then add the prawns. Mix briefly, so the prawns are fully coated, then cover and chill for at least 30 minutes, or overnight.

Prepare the BBQ. If using bamboo skewers, soak them in water for at least 10 minutes, until saturated, to avoid them burning on the heat.

Thread 4–6 prawns on to each skewer, then place them on the BBQ over a high heat. Cook them for 2–3 minutes, until they are coloured on one side, then turn and cook the other side.

Remove from the grill. To serve, squeeze lemon juice over each skewer and sprinkle with chopped coriander.

MAKES:
4 skewers

INGREDIENTS
Sweet chilli marinade
  (see page 79)
150 g king prawns,
  peeled
1 lemon, cut into
  wedges
Coriander, chopped

GRILLED TROUT WITH NEW POTATOES AND CHERRY TOMATOES

Easy, healthy, fresh, delicious – need I say more?

METHOD

Place the lemon slices and the sprigs of dill into the cavity of the fish and set to one side.

Bring a saucepan of water and the teaspoon of salt to the boil and cook the potatoes in it for 10 minutes. Drain, allow to dry, then transfer to a bowl and toss them in 1 tbsp olive oil. Set to one side.

Prepare the BBQ.

Gently brush the outside of the fish with the remaining oil, then place on the grill over a low heat. Cook for 6–7 minutes on each side, until the skin is browned.

After you turn the fish, put the cherry tomatoes directly onto the grill over a medium heat (if small, skewer them so that they don't fall through). Cook for 5–6 minutes, turning occasionally, until the skins are blistered.

While these cook, add the potatoes to the grill over a medium heat, and cook for 5 minutes, turning occasionally.

Serve everything immediately.

INGREDIENTS

1 lemon, sliced
3 sprigs dill
1 trout, gutted
  and cleaned
1 tsp salt
250 g new potatoes
2 tbsp olive oil
250 g cherry tomatoes

BBQ SCALLOPS

Believe it or not, this fancy dish is simple to make (but don't tell your friends).

METHOD

Brush the scallops lightly with oil, and season with salt and pepper to taste.

Prepare the BBQ.

Place the scallops on a medium–high heat and cook for 3 minutes. Then turn them over and cook for another 3 minutes, until the scallops are golden in colour and warm all the way through.

Remove from the grill and drizzle with lemon juice.

Serve on a bed of asparagus and top with pea shoots if desired.

INGREDIENTS

4 large scallops
1 tbsp olive oil
Pinch salt
Pinch ground
  black pepper
2 tbsp lemon juice
Asparagus and pea
  shoots, to serve
  (optional)

CEDAR-SMOKED SALMON

For this recipe you will need a grill with a lid and a large cedar grilling plank (or two smaller ones), which can be purchased online. You will also need a spray bottle filled with water handy.

METHOD

Before cooking, soak the cedar plank(s) for 1–2 hours, until wet through.

Whisk together the oil, salt, peppercorns, lemon zest, lemon juice and parsley in a shallow dish. Add the salmon, stir to coat, then leave to marinate at room temperature for 30 minutes.

Prepare the BBQ.

Place the cedar plank on a medium heat and wait until it starts to smoke and crackle. If the plank catches fire, spray the wood with a little water.

Place the salmon on to the plank and close the lid. Cook for 15–20 minutes. When the fish is done, it will be flaky when you scrape it with a fork.

Remove both the plank and the salmon carefully from the grill, transfer the salmon to a plate and serve immediately.

SERVES: 2

INGREDIENTS
2 tbsp olive oil
Pinch salt
1 tsp peppercorns
Zest of 1 lemon
2 tsp lemon juice
Small bunch parsley, chopped finely
2 salmon fillets

GRILLED HALLOUMI BURGER WITH YOGURT MINT SAUCE

This halloumi burger is juicy, salty and fresh, with a cooling hit of yogurt mint sauce to top it off.

METHOD

Slice the tomato and onion thinly, wash and dry any salad greens and cut the burger buns in half. Set to one side.

Prepare the sauce. Add the yogurt, mint sauce and salt to a bowl and stir to combine. Adjust levels of mint sauce and salt to taste.

If using a block of halloumi, slice it into 1 cm slices. Brush the slices lightly with olive oil.

Prepare the BBQ.

Place the halloumi slices over the hottest part of the grill. Cook on each side for 30 seconds at a time. Keep turning until char lines appear on each side.

Layer the salad, halloumi, tomato, onion and sauce in the burger buns and serve. Garnish with chopped mint leaves if desired.

MAKES: 2 burgers

INGREDIENTS
For the burgers:
1 large tomato
1 large red onion
Handful lettuce, or other
  salad leaves of choice
2 burger buns
225-g block of halloumi, or
  4 halloumi burger slices
2 tbsp olive oil
Mint leaves, chopped, to
  garnish (optional)

For the yogurt mint sauce:
6 tbsp plain yogurt (or a
  non-dairy alternative)
2-3 tsp mint sauce
Pinch salt

ASIAN TOFU BURGER

With saltiness, sweetness, spiciness and a good mouthful of crunch, this veggie burger has got it all.

METHOD

Cut the tofu in half, so that you have two square patties.

Whisk the soy sauce, five spice, oil, sugar and garlic in a shallow dish, then add the tofu and turn them to coat. Cover and refrigerate for an hour.

Prepare the BBQ.

Place the tofu patties over a medium–high heat and cook for 10–12 minutes on each side. Move them to the low heat area of the grill when done to keep warm.

When the tofu is nearly done, bring a saucepan of water to the boil. Add the beansprouts, cook for 1 minute, then drain and set to one side.

Slice the buns in half and place each half flat-side down on the grill over a medium heat. Cook for 2 minutes, or until the buns are lightly toasted.

Assemble the burgers: layer the green salad, tofu, tomato and beansprouts in the bun and serve.

MAKES: 2 burgers

INGREDIENTS

400 g extra-firm tofu
2 tbsp soy sauce
½ tsp five-spice powder
1 tbsp olive or sesame oil
1 tsp brown sugar
2 cloves garlic, minced
Handful beansprouts
2 vegan brioche buns or vegan burger buns
1 tomato, sliced
Handful green salad, washed and dried

CHEESY PORTOBELLO MUSHROOMS

This simple dish packs a fantastic flavour punch with garlic, soy sauce and cheese.

METHOD

Melt the butter in a small pan, then add the onion and garlic. Cook over a medium heat until the onions are translucent, and the garlic fragrant (a few minutes). Remove from the pan and set to one side.

Wash the mushrooms and pat them dry. Remove the stems. Lightly brush the mushrooms all over with oil and set to one side. Prepare the BBQ.

Place the mushrooms on a medium–high heat, gills facing up, and cook for 3 minutes, then turn them over and cook for a further 2 minutes.

Transfer the mushrooms to a plate, and drizzle lightly with soy sauce. Top each one with onion and garlic, and finish with a layer of grated cheese. Return the mushrooms to the grill over a medium heat and cook for a further 5 minutes, until the mushrooms are heated through and the cheese has melted.

Serve immediately, garnished with parsley if desired.

MAKES:
4 stuffed mushrooms

INGREDIENTS

1 small knob butter
1 small onion, minced
2 cloves garlic, minced
4 portobello
  mushrooms
1 tbsp olive oil
2 tbsp soy sauce
50 g Cheddar
  cheese, grated
Curly-leaf parsley, to
  garnish (optional)

GRILLED AVOCADO STUFFED WITH TOMATOES AND RICOTTA CHEESE

Take your avocados to the next level with this delicious ricotta cheese and tomato salsa recipe.

METHOD

Dice the tomatoes and add to a bowl along with the minced garlic and 1 tsp of the lime juice. Stir to combine and add salt to taste. Add more lime juice if desired, but make sure you reserve at least 1 tsp of it. Set the salsa to one side. (For extra-strong flavour, you can make the salsa up to a day in advance and leave it to chill in the fridge until needed.)

Prepare the BBQ.

Cut the avocados in half and remove the stones. Drizzle the halves with the remaining lime juice, then brush each one lightly with oil.

Place the avocados flat-side down on the grill over a high heat for 2–3 minutes, or until you can see char marks on the flesh.

Remove from the grill, spoon salsa into the middle, top with ricotta cheese and serve.

MAKES:
4 avocado halves

INGREDIENTS
3 large, ripe tomatoes
1 clove garlic, minced
Juice of 1 lime
Salt, to taste
2 avocados
1 tbsp olive oil
50 g ricotta cheese, crumbled

MIXED VEGETABLE AND BBQ SEITAN SKEWERS

Never underestimate the deliciousness of vegan food.

METHOD

Combine the ingredients for the BBQ sauce in a small saucepan and stir over a medium heat until the sugar is dissolved and the sauce is thick. Adjust the seasoning to taste, remove from the heat and set to one side.

Chop the seitan into bite-sized chunks and place in a large, shallow dish. Coat well with the BBQ sauce, then cover and allow to marinate at room temperature for at least 1 hour.

Chop the courgette into rounds, approx. 1 cm in thickness. Cut the top off each pepper and remove the seeds. Then set the vegetables to one side.

Prepare the BBQ. If using bamboo skewers, soak them in water for at least 10 minutes, until saturated, to avoid them burning on the heat.

Thread the seitan, courgette and peppers on to the skewers. Grill on a medium–high heat for 8–10 minutes, turning occasionally, or until char marks appear.

Serve immediately.

MAKES:
6–8 skewers

INGREDIENTS
For the BBQ sauce:
8 tbsp ketchup
2 tbsp vegan Worcestershire sauce
2 tbsp dark brown sugar
1 tbsp vegan red wine vinegar
1 tsp garlic granules
¼ tsp cayenne pepper
¼ tsp paprika
¼ tsp salt
¼ tsp ground black pepper

For the skewers:
225 g seitan
1 small courgette
16 mini peppers

GRILLED CAULIFLOWER STEAK

This cauliflower king proves that steaks aren't just for the meat eaters!

METHOD

Wash the cauliflower, remove the leaves and trim the stem so that the bottom is flat. Then cut the cauliflower down the middle into two "steaks". This will be easiest with a large, sharp knife.

Mix the oil, lime juice, honey and garlic in a bowl. In a separate bowl, mix the paprika, turmeric, cumin, coriander and salt.

Prepare the BBQ.

Lightly brush one side of each steak with the oil mixture, then sprinkle the spices on top (reserving some for the other side). Place each steak oil-side down over a medium–high heat and cook for 4–5 minutes.

While cooking, brush the uncoated tops lightly with oil and sprinkle on the remainder of the seasoning.

When char marks appear on the first side, turn the cauliflower over and cook for another 4–5 minutes.

Serve immediately.

SERVES: 2

INGREDIENTS
1 large cauliflower
2 tbsp olive oil
Juice of 1 lime
1 tsp runny honey
2 cloves garlic, minced
1 tbsp paprika
½ tsp turmeric
¼ tsp cumin
½ tsp ground coriander
½ tsp salt

SAUCES, MARINADES AND RUBS

Whisky glaze • Chunky tomato sauce • Sweet chilli marinade • Homemade mayonnaise • Avocado, lime and coriander dressing • Rosemary, garlic and lemon salad dressing • Honey mustard salad dressing • Cajun rub • Lemon and herb rub • Tandoori rub • Asian rub • BBQ rub

WHISKY GLAZE

Slather this glaze over ribs, steak, salmon or tofu.

METHOD

Combine all the ingredients in a small saucepan over a low heat. Stir for 3–5 minutes, or until the sugar has dissolved and the sauce has thickened slightly.

Adjust seasoning to taste.

Use immediately, or allow to cool and refrigerate in an airtight container for up to a week.

MAKES:
approx. 150 ml

INGREDIENTS
120 ml whisky
5 tbsp ketchup
50 g brown sugar
15 g non-dairy
    margarine
2 cloves garlic, minced
2 tbsp cider vinegar
½ tbsp lemon juice
1 tsp soy sauce
¼ tsp salt
¼ tsp ground
    black pepper

CHUNKY TOMATO SAUCE

Make this rich tomato sauce a day ahead of when you need it. Perfect for nachos or as a juicy burger accompaniment.

METHOD

Heat the oil in a saucepan over a medium heat. Add the onion and garlic, and cook until fragrant, for 3–5 minutes.

Add the tomato purée and cook for another minute.

Add the chopped tomatoes, brown sugar, salt and pepper and stir to combine. Bring to the boil, and then reduce to a simmer and cook for 15–20 minutes. The sauce should reduce by a half and thicken.

Stir in the butter and adjust the seasoning to taste.

Allow the sauce to cool, before transferring to an airtight container. Refrigerate until needed. Use within 3 days. Serve at room temperature.

MAKES:
approx. 200 g, or
   1 small bowl of sauce

INGREDIENTS
1 tbsp olive oil
½ small onion,
   chopped
2 cloves garlic, minced
1 tbsp tomato purée
400-g can chopped
   tomatoes
1 tbsp dark
   brown sugar
1 tsp salt
¼ tsp ground
   black pepper
1 knob non-dairy
   margarine

SWEET CHILLI MARINADE

This marinade is a sweet and spicy winner for all your BBQ favourites, including prawns, chicken, pork ribs and salads.

METHOD

In a large bowl, whisk the sweet chilli sauce, lime juice, soy sauce, garlic, ginger and sugar together until smooth.

Adjust to taste, adding more lime, sugar or chilli sauce as desired.

If you want your marinade to be extra spicy, slice up a red chilli, retaining the seeds, add it to the bowl and stir briefly to combine.

If not using the marinade straight away, decant it into an airtight container and keep refrigerated for up to 2 weeks.

MAKES:
approx. 200 ml

INGREDIENTS
150 ml sweet
   chilli sauce
Juice of 1 lime
3 tbsp soy sauce
3 cloves garlic, minced
1 cm ginger, grated
1 tsp brown sugar,
   to taste
1 red chilli (optional)

HOMEMADE MAYONNAISE

Impress your friends and family by whipping up your very own mayo.

METHOD

Add the eggs, mustard, lemon juice and vinegar to a food processor and pulse until combined. If you don't have a food processor, add ingredients to a bowl and mix with a fork or balloon whisk.

Add the oil a tablespoon at a time, pulsing (or whisking thoroughly) between each addition. When the mixture thickens slightly, repeat the process until you have added all the oil.

Add salt to taste, adjust any other seasoning if desired and mix again.

If the mayonnaise is not yet the desired thickness, keep the food processor running (or keep whisking) while adding more oil a tablespoon at a time until it is to your liking.

Store in an airtight container in the fridge for up to a week.

MAKES:
approx. 500 ml

INGREDIENTS
2 eggs, whisked
2 tbsp Dijon mustard
2 tsp lemon juice
1 tbsp white wine
   vinegar
440 ml vegetable,
   sunflower or olive oil
Salt, to taste

AVOCADO, LIME AND CORIANDER DRESSING

Drizzle this creamy dressing over veggies and salads.

METHOD

Put the avocados, olive oil, coriander, lime juice, lime zest and garlic cloves in a food processor and pulse until smooth. Alternatively, add ingredients to a small bowl and blitz with a hand-held stick blender.

If it is too thick, add water a teaspoon at a time until you reach the desired consistency.

Add salt and pepper to taste.

Store in an airtight container in the fridge for up to 3 days.

MAKES:

approx. 500 ml

INGREDIENTS

2 small avocados,
   peeled and pitted
120 ml olive oil
4 tbsp fresh coriander
Juice and zest
   of 2 limes
2 cloves garlic, minced
Salt, to taste
Ground black
   pepper, to taste

ROSEMARY, GARLIC AND LEMON SALAD DRESSING

Try this fragrant dressing on the pomegranate and raisin couscous (see page 107).

METHOD

Add the peppercorns, salt, rosemary and garlic to a mortar and use the pestle to crush it into a paste.

Add the lemon juice and continue mashing to combine.

Transfer to a sealable container and add the olive oil. Seal the lid, and shake the dressing until mixed.

Add the extra sprig of rosemary, if desired, and store in the fridge for up to 5 days.

MAKES:
approx. 80 ml

INGREDIENTS

¼ tsp black peppercorns

½ tsp salt, or to taste

2 sprigs rosemary, stems removed (plus an extra sprig for a garnish, if desired)

2 cloves garlic

2 tbsp lemon juice

60 ml olive oil

HONEY MUSTARD SALAD DRESSING

Use this versatile sauce as a dressing for a crisp salad, a dip for your veggies or even a marinade.

METHOD

Whisk together all the ingredients in a small bowl until well combined.

Refrigerate in an airtight container and use within 5 days.

MAKES:
approx. 70 ml

INGREDIENTS
2 tbsp runny honey
2 tbsp Dijon mustard
2 tbsp apple
  cider vinegar
40 ml olive oil
1 clove garlic, minced
¼ tsp salt, or to taste
¼ tsp ground black
  pepper, or to taste

CAJUN RUB

Try this rub on chicken, steak and burgers, or sprinkled on potatoes.

 MAKES: approx. 12 tsp

INGREDIENTS
1½ tbsp paprika
2 tsp garlic granules
1 tsp salt
1 tsp dried oregano
1 tsp dried thyme
1 tsp ground black pepper
½ tsp cayenne pepper
½ tsp onion powder
½ tsp caster sugar

METHOD
Put all the ingredients into a bowl and mix well.

Store in an airtight container in a cool, dry place for up to 3 months.

LEMON AND HERB RUB

This is perfect for chicken, fish and potatoes.

 MAKES: approx. 6 tsp

INGREDIENTS
1 tbsp ground black pepper
1 tsp oregano
1 tsp thyme
Zest of 1 lemon
½ tsp salt
½ tsp garlic granules

METHOD
Put all the ingredients into a bowl and mix well.

Store in an airtight container in a cool, dry place for up to 2 days.

TANDOORI RUB

This spice blend works well on chicken, fish and tofu.

 MAKES: approx. 6 tsp

INGREDIENTS
1 tsp paprika
1 tsp ground ginger
1 tsp turmeric
1 tsp salt
¾ tsp ground black pepper
½ tsp cumin
½ tsp ground coriander
¼ tsp caster sugar

METHOD
Put all the ingredients into a bowl and mix well.

Store in an airtight container in a cool, dry place for up to 3 months.

ASIAN RUB

Use this on chicken and pork, or veggie kebabs.

 MAKES: approx. 8 tsp

INGREDIENTS
2 tbsp five-spice powder
1 tsp garlic granules
½ tsp ground black pepper
½ tsp brown sugar
½ tsp salt

METHOD
Put all the ingredients into a bowl and mix well.

Store in an airtight container in a cool, dry place for up to 3 months.

BBQ RUB

Apply liberally to chicken, pork, beef or tofu for a classic BBQ flavour.

 MAKES: approx. 8 tsp

INGREDIENTS

1 tbsp brown sugar
1 tbsp smoked paprika
½ tsp garlic granules
½ tsp cayenne pepper
½ tsp ground black pepper
½ tsp cumin
¼ tbsp salt
Pinch ground allspice

METHOD

Put all the ingredients into a bowl and mix well.

Store in an airtight container in a cool, dry place for up to 3 months.

SIDE DISHES

Potato salad with mustard seeds • Mango salsa • Creamy coleslaw • Camembert fondue • Green salad with mozzarella, sun-dried tomatoes and lemon dressing • Seared aubergine and quinoa salad • Pomegranate and raisin couscous • Feta, broccoli, tomato and olive pasta salad • Super green salad • Corn on the cob with fire butter • Loaded nachos

POTATO SALAD WITH MUSTARD SEEDS

Make this simple potato salad a couple of hours ahead of your BBQ for best results.

METHOD

Wash the potatoes and chop them into bite-sized pieces. Bring a pan of water to the boil and boil the potatoes for 10 minutes, or until they can be pierced with a blunt knife. Drain and set to one side to cool.

Once the potatoes are cool, put them in a large bowl along with the mayonnaise, sour cream, mustard, mustard seeds, garlic granules and dill. Mix until everything is combined and the potatoes are well coated.

Season with salt and pepper to taste, and adjust the levels of mustard, mayo and garlic to your liking. Cover and refrigerate for at least an hour before serving.

Potato salad keeps for up to 2 days in the fridge.

SERVES:
3-4 as a side

INGREDIENTS
500 g new potatoes
2 tbsp mayonnaise
1 tbsp sour cream
1 tsp wholegrain mustard
1 tsp mustard seeds
1 tsp garlic granules
2 tbsp fresh dill, chopped
Salt, to taste
Ground black pepper, to taste

MANGO SALSA

This salsa adds a tropical twist to any dish.

METHOD

Put all the ingredients into a bowl and mix well, until combined.

Cover and refrigerate for at least 30 minutes before serving, as this will let the flavours develop.

SERVES:
6-8 as a side

INGREDIENTS

1 mango, peeled, pitted and diced
½ red onion, diced
2 jalapeños (red and green), deseeded and diced
1 red pepper, deseeded and chopped
Handful fresh coriander leaves, chopped
Juice of 1 lime
Pinch caster sugar
Pinch salt

CREAMY COLESLAW

The perfect side for burgers, fish, chicken, kebabs – you name it!

METHOD

Wash the cabbage and chop into shreds, grate the carrots and chop the spring onions finely. Add all the vegetables to a large bowl.

In a small bowl, mix the mayonnaise, mustard, vinegar and sugar until combined. Then add this to the vegetables and toss until well coated.

Season with pepper to taste, and adjust the levels of mayonnaise to your liking.

Serve immediately, or cover and refrigerate for up to 2 days.

SERVES:
3-4 as a side

INGREDIENTS
½ cabbage (green or purple)
4 carrots
4 spring onions
4 tbsp mayonnaise
1 tsp wholegrain mustard
1 tsp cider vinegar
½ tsp caster sugar
Pepper, to taste

CAMEMBERT FONDUE

Dig crusty bread into this magnificent wheel of silky, melted cheese. Mmm...

METHOD
Prepare the BBQ.

Remove any packaging from the Camembert, reserving the wooden box.

Place the cheese back in the bottom half of the box (don't add the lid) and scatter the top with rosemary and thyme.

Wrap the boxed cheese loosely in a layer of baking paper, then a layer of foil, and place over a low heat on the grill for 10–15 minutes, or until the cheese is soft and liquid in the centre.

Serve immediately, with hunks of crusty bread if desired.

INGREDIENTS
1 wheel unpasteurized Camembert in a wooden tub
3 fresh rosemary sprigs (approx.)
3 fresh thyme sprigs (approx.)
Crusty bread, to serve (optional)

GREEN SALAD WITH MOZZARELLA, SUN-DRIED TOMATOES AND LEMON DRESSING

Salad sometimes takes a back seat at BBQs – but not this one. It's colourful, juicy, full of flavour and oh so simple to make.

METHOD

To make the salad, wash and drain the salad leaves, then add them to a large bowl. Add the sun-dried tomatoes (chopped into bite-sized pieces if they are not already small) and the red onion. Then tear the mozzarella ball into smaller pieces and add each one to the bowl. Toss the salad to combine.

Add the salad dressing a tablespoon at a time and mix until you feel that the salad is suitably dressed.

Serve the salad straight away, or store for up to a day, covered, in the fridge.

SERVES:
3-4 as a side

INGREDIENTS
120 g salad leaves
100 g sun-dried
   tomatoes
½ red onion, sliced
1 large ball mozzarella
2-3 tbsp rosemary,
   garlic and lemon
   salad dressing
   (see page 85)

SEARED AUBERGINE AND QUINOA SALAD

If you just can't get enough of your grill, why not BBQ your salad as well?

METHOD

Put the quinoa in a sieve and rinse in cold water until the water running off is clear. Then bring 250 ml water to the boil in a saucepan. Add the quinoa and cook for 12–15 minutes, or until the water has been absorbed and the grains are double their original size. Drain any remaining water, set to one side and allow to cool.

Add the cooled quinoa to a large bowl with the lettuce and chilli. Drizzle the salad dressing over, a little at a time, and toss to coat. Add more salad dressing if desired. Cover and chill until needed, for up to 2 days.

Prepare the BBQ.

Cut the top and bottom off the aubergine and discard, then slice the rest into 1.5 cm slices. Brush each slice lightly with olive oil and season with salt and pepper to taste.

Grill over a medium heat for 4–5 minutes on each side, or until char marks appear.

Serve the aubergine slices on top of the quinoa salad.

SERVES:
3-4 as a side

INGREDIENTS

For the salad:
100 g quinoa
3-4 large lettuce
  leaves, shredded
1 red chilli, deseeded
  and chopped
30 ml rosemary,
  garlic and lemon
  salad dressing
  (see page 85)

For the aubergine:
1 aubergine
3 tbsp olive oil
Salt, to taste
Ground black
  pepper, to taste

POMEGRANATE AND RAISIN COUSCOUS

Add a fruity pop to your BBQ spread with this simple side dish.

METHOD

Soak the raisins in warm water for 30 minutes. Drain and set to one side.

Put the couscous in a bowl and pour over 200 ml boiling water, then cover. After 5 minutes, fluff up the grains with a fork. Leave to cool.

In a large bowl, add the couscous, raisins and pomegranate seeds and mix briefly. Then drizzle the salad dressing over, a little at a time. Toss to combine and add more dressing if desired.

Cover and refrigerate until needed, or for up to 2 days.

SERVES:
3-4 as a side

INGREDIENTS
50 g raisins
200 g couscous
100 g pomegranate
 seeds
30 ml honey mustard
 salad dressing
 (see page 87)

FETA, BROCCOLI, TOMATO AND OLIVE PASTA SALAD

A pasta salad will always go down well with the crowds – so try this Mediterranean-themed recipe!

METHOD

Bring a large pan of water to the boil and add the salt. Cook the pasta as per the packet instructions and drain. Add the pasta to a large bowl, toss with ½ tbsp olive oil and allow to cool.

Chop the broccoli into small florets. Bring another pan of water to the boil, add the broccoli and cook for 6–8 minutes, or until the stalks can be pierced by a blunt knife. Drain and allow to cool.

Add the broccoli, tomatoes, olives and feta cheese to the pasta bowl and toss briefly to mix. Add the rest of the olive oil and the balsamic vinegar to taste, and toss again until the salad is evenly coated.

Cover and refrigerate until needed, for up to 2 days.

SERVES:
2-3 as a side

INGREDIENTS
1 tsp salt
100 g radiatori pasta (or your pasta of choice)
1½ tbsp olive oil, or to taste
½ head broccoli
12 cherry tomatoes, quartered
12 black olives, pitted
100 g feta cheese, chopped into chunks
1 tbsp balsamic vinegar, or to taste

SUPER GREEN SALAD

If superfood is your thing, you'll love this salad!

METHOD

Put the quinoa in a sieve and rinse in cold water until the water running off is clear. Then bring 250 ml water to the boil in a saucepan. Add the quinoa and cook for 12–15 minutes, or until the water has been absorbed and the grains are double their original size. Drain any remaining water, set to one side and allow to cool.

Bring another pan of water to the boil and add the chickpeas. Cook for 5 minutes, drain and set aside to cool.

In a small bowl, whisk the olive oil, lemon juice, vegan red wine vinegar, sugar, salt and pepper.

In a large bowl, add the quinoa, chickpeas, kale and onion and mix briefly. Then drizzle the salad dressing over, a little at a time. Toss to combine and add more dressing and the basil leaves if desired.

Cover and refrigerate until needed, or for up to 2 days.

SERVES:
3-4 as a side

INGREDIENTS
100 g quinoa
400-g tin chickpeas, drained
1 tbsp olive oil
Juice of 1 lemon
1 tsp vegan red wine vinegar
½ tsp caster sugar
Pinch salt, to taste
Pinch ground black pepper, to taste
70 g kale, chopped finely
½ red onion, sliced thinly
Basil leaves, to garnish (optional)

CORN ON THE COB WITH FIRE BUTTER

Make this spicy chilli butter if you dare...

METHOD

Wash and dry each corncob and remove any leaves. Wrap each cob loosely in two sheets of foil and set to one side.

Chop the chilli finely, keeping the seeds if you would like the butter to be extra spicy (discard them if not).

In a small bowl, add the softened butter, chopped chilli, chilli flakes, paprika and cayenne pepper. Mix until well combined and adjust the chilli levels to your liking. Cover and set to one side.

Prepare the BBQ.

Add the foil-wrapped corncobs over a low heat and grill for 25–30 minutes, turning occasionally.

Serve immediately with the chilli butter on the side.

MAKES: 4 corncobs

INGREDIENTS

4 corncobs
60 g butter, softened
1 red chilli
1 tsp chilli flakes
½ tsp paprika
¼ tsp cayenne pepper

LOADED NACHOS

Nachos are a tried-and-tested party favourite (and the perfect snack while you wait for the burgers!).

METHOD

Add the tortilla chips to a large, shallow dish. Add the chillies and avocado and mix briefly to combine.

Top with tomato sauce and a generous dollop of sour cream, and fresh coriander if desired.

Serve immediately.

SERVES:
2-4 as a side

INGREDIENTS

200 g tortilla chips
2 green chillies, sliced
1 avocado, peeled, pitted and chopped into chunks
4 tbsp chunky tomato sauce (see page 77)
2 tbsp sour cream
Fresh coriander (optional)

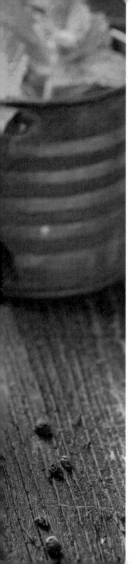

SWEET TREATS

Marshmallow and strawberry kebabs • Grilled Lady Finger bananas with salted caramel sauce • Grilled apple and salted caramel sandwich • Boozy BBQ pineapple • Grilled pound cake with fresh berries and whipped cream

MARSHMALLOW AND STRAWBERRY KEBABS

Soft, pillowy marshmallows and sharp, fresh strawberries. You're welcome.

METHOD
Prepare the BBQ.

If using bamboo skewers, soak them in water for at least 10 minutes, until saturated, to avoid them burning on the heat.

Thread three marshmallows and two strawberries alternately on to each skewer.

Place over a low–medium heat, turning every 20–30 seconds, until grill marks begin to appear on the marshmallows.

Serve immediately, with cookies and chocolate sauce if desired.

INGREDIENTS
15 large marshmallows
10 strawberries,
   hulled if preferred
Cookies (optional)
Chocolate sauce
   (optional)

GRILLED LADY FINGER BANANAS WITH SALTED CARAMEL SAUCE

If you can't find any Lady Finger bananas, small, regular bananas will be delicious with this recipe too.

METHOD

Add all the sauce ingredients to a small pan over a low heat. Stir gently until the sugar has dissolved. Then increase the heat, bring the mixture to the boil and keep it bubbling for 2–3 minutes, or until the sauce has thickened. Remove from the heat and set to one side to cool, uncovered. Prepare the BBQ.

Cut out six squares of kitchen foil, approx. 15 cm (6 in.) squared. Lightly grease each sheet of foil with butter.

Peel the bananas and wrap each one loosely in the foil. Then bake the bananas on a low heat for 10 minutes, or until the bananas are soft. Remove from the heat.

If the caramel sauce has cooled too much, reheat it gently over a low heat, stirring continuously, until it is hot through.

When the foil is cool enough to touch, serve the bananas immediately, topped with salted caramel sauce. Any spare sauce can be refrigerated in an airtight container for up to 3 days.

MAKES: 6 bananas

INGREDIENTS

For the salted caramel sauce:
230 ml double cream
130 g light brown sugar
1 tbsp dark brown sugar
40 g butter
½ tsp vanilla essence
½ tsp salt, or to taste

For the bananas:
6 Lady Finger bananas
1 tbsp butter

GRILLED APPLE AND SALTED CARAMEL SANDWICH

This sweet snack is like autumn in a sandwich – but suitable all year round.

METHOD

Prepare the BBQ.

Take four slices of bread, butter them, sprinkle lightly with brown sugar and cinnamon and set to one side.

Cut the apple into large, thin slices and sprinkle both sides lightly with caster sugar. Place the apple slices on the grill over a medium heat. Grill for a minute or so on each side, until grill marks begin to appear. Remove from the heat and set to one side.

To assemble each sandwich, take a slice of bread, layer it with apple slices and top with another slice of bread.

Lightly butter the outsides of both sandwiches, then place them over a medium heat. Grill until the bread is crisp and grill marks begin to appear. Turn the sandwiches over and repeat on the other side.

Serve immediately with a drizzle of salted caramel sauce.

MAKES:
2 sandwiches

INGREDIENTS
4 slices white bread
2 tbsp butter (approx.)
1 tbsp brown sugar
1 tbsp ground
   cinnamon
1 large apple
   (any variety)
1 tbsp caster sugar
Salted caramel
   sauce (see page
   121), to serve

BOOZY BBQ PINEAPPLE

Although delicious on their own, these tipsy pineapple slices are best served with scoops of vanilla ice cream and long summer evenings.

METHOD

Add the rum, brown sugar and mixed spice to a pan over a low heat, and stir until the sugar has dissolved. Remove from the heat.

Drain the pineapple slices and place them in a wide, shallow bowl or dish. Pour the rum mixture over the pineapple, cover and leave to marinate for at least 30 minutes, or up to 3 hours.

Prepare the BBQ.

Remove the pineapples from the marinade and shake briefly to ensure that they are not dripping.

Add the pineapple slices over a high heat and cook on each side for 1–2 minutes, until char marks appear.

Serve immediately.

SERVES: 3-4

INGREDIENTS

200 ml dark rum
80 g brown sugar
1 tsp mixed spice
220-g tin pineapple
  slices

GRILLED POUND CAKE WITH FRESH BERRIES AND WHIPPED CREAM

This American classic of delicate, buttery pound cake is made even better by throwing it on the barbie.

METHOD

Preheat oven to 180°C/360°F/gas mark 4. Then grease a 900-g (2-lb) loaf tin and line it with baking paper.

In a large bowl, cream the butter and the sugar together with an electric mixer until it's very pale and fluffy. This will take several minutes.

Add the eggs one at a time, mixing well between each addition. Then gradually stir in the flour by hand, a little at a time. Finally, stir in the lemon zest, vanilla and salt.

Pour the batter into the loaf tin and bake for 20 minutes, or until a skewer inserted into the middle of the cake comes out clean. Once done, leave on a rack until fully cool.

Prepare the BBQ.

Cut the cake into slices. Spread butter on both sides of each slice before placing them over a medium heat. Grill on each side for 1–2 minutes.

Serve immediately with the berries and cream.

SERVES: 10-12

INGREDIENTS

280 g butter, plus
  extra for greasing
  and spreading
300 g caster sugar
3 large eggs
300 g plain flour
Zest of 1 lemon
1½ tsp vanilla extract
½ tsp salt
250 g fresh mixed
  berries, to serve
Whipped cream,
  to serve

Have you enjoyed this book?
If so, find us on Facebook at **Summersdale Publishers**,
on Twitter/X at **@Summersdale** and on Instagram and TikTok at
@summersdalebooks and get in touch. We'd love to hear from you!

www.summersdale.com

Image credits